GOD & HIP HOP

A 21-Day Biblical Devotion Inspired By Hip-Hop

By: ·
Ayanna Mills Gallow

God and Hip Hop
Copyright © 2019 by Ayanna Mills Gallow

FIRST EDITION
Book design by Allison Arnett of www.branditbeautifully.com

ISBN 978-0-578-50051-5

Scriptures are from the King James Bible unless otherwise indicated.

BOOK'S INSPIRATION & PURPOSE:

- Growing up on Independence Avenue in Freeport, NY, going to church was not a weekly thing for my family and most families that I knew. There were a few families I knew that lived what I would consider today as the Christian life, but I wasn't fully introduced to the Lord and Christianity until I went to Temple University in Philadelphia, PA for college. After moving back to New York, on Palm Sunday in 2001, I gave my life to the Lord at Little Zion Church in Freeport, NY. I was right back where I started, but older and wiser.

- Everything happens at Godspeed, but at one point I was searching for religion, but I didn't know where to turn. I would say, "What does it mean to be saved and how do I do that?" Therefore, it is important to me to make sure I am speaking of the Lord to help any people who are searching for Him like I was.

- As a child, I had music to help shape my thoughts. I fell in love with hip hop music when I was 11 years old. My childhood friend, Cerrone Sherrod, and I would watch Video Music Box and wait for, "Self-Destruction's" video to come on. "Self- Destruction" is a collaborative song with some outstanding lyricist and it is still my favorite song today.

- I enjoy Hip Hop Music because of the beats and positive messages and I enjoy Gospel Music because of the motivation and spiritual connection. I didn't have a big spiritual connection when I was younger, but I had a love for music. Therefore, I want this book to inspire the musical people and help develop a closer spiritual connection with God.

BOOK DEDICATION: TO MY WINNING HAND

My Ace in a Hole: Ma, the older I get the more I realize the sacrifices you made for us. Your life gave me life & strength. I wouldn't be able to do half of what I can if I didn't have you. I vow to honor you for all of my days. I love you always.

My 4 Queens + Wild Card: Nanny, Tia, Debra, Ticky (RIP) and Alterrell Mills Sr., I appreciate you for making me the woman I am today.

My King of Spade: Louis Sterling King, you were the final piece to my puzzle and I thank God for you.

My 2 Kings: CJ & Camron – Although I didn't birth you, my love for you is endless. Although we live apart, you are always in my thoughts and in my heart.

My 3 Ace's: Keeb, Mez & Tay: You 3 make me be a better me and I love our bond. Thank you for always being there. I love you tremendously.

My King of Heart: Through my ups and downs, thank you for your inspiration, encouragement, and love.

My Deuce of Diamonds & Deuce of Spades: Cydnee, Jani, Deuce, Andre, Ceyma, and Nasir– You all inspire and I am thankful that your mothers allowed me to be a part of your lives. I love you very much.

My 10 for 2: Colby & Caleb– Your mere existence makes me strive every day. Whether I am in front of you to lead the way, next to you for support, or behind you to push you forward to reach for the stars, I plan to be there every step of the way by the grace of God. My life is dedicated to you. Mom Love Forever & Beyond.

TABLE OF CONTENTS

TRACK 1

GOD'S BLUEPRINT

GOD'S BLUEPRINT

*C*an you go to, "The End of The Road" or, are you, "Ready To Die?" Does your mind say, "I'm Going Down," or, "I Believe I Can Fly?" If you could describe your life based on a theme song, what would it be?

"For I know the plans I have for you," declares the Lord, *"plans to prosper you and not to harm you, plans to give you hope and a future."* (Jeremiah 29:11 NIV)

Do you ever feel like you are just here and not really living? Do you feel hopeless and wonder how you will do this thing called life? You are not alone because God is here for you and He has the blueprint for your life. God created you for His plan and purpose to prosper you. He wants you to feel good inside and outside. You have to know who you are to discover your full potential.

God can bring you through all the pain, circumstances, limitations and fear. Your life was designed to be lived to the fullest with abundance. However, if you do not realize it, then it's like having $1,000,000 in the bank, but begging for food because you don't know you have it. God wants you here so don't give up. If you aren't living your prosperous life, then it's time for a makeover and a closer walk with God. *"Come near to God and he will come near to you."* (James 4:8 NIV)

Let's get closer to God to uncover His blueprint.

"Be the best of whatever you are. And finally, and finally, in your life's blueprint, must be a commitment to the eternal principles of

beauty, love, and justice." Martin Luther King, Jr. What is Your Life's Blueprint? (Broadside)

Prayer: Father thank you for my life. Please give me the spirit of wisdom and revelation in the knowledge of you so that my eyes will be enlightened and I will know you better and the rich inheritance that you have for your people. In Jesus Name.

_____

_____

_____

_____

_____

_____

_____

_____

_____

_____

_____

_____

_____

_____

_____

_____

_____

_____

_____

_____

_____

_____

_____

_____

TRACK 2

NOW WHAT?

NOW WHAT?

*D*o you trust God enough to tell Him your dreams? Are you afraid to ask for things because you don't think you deserve them? God says, *"You may ask anything in my name and I will do it."* (John 14:14 NIV)

God has given us a clean slate and a blank check. We have to get before God, and get acquainted with His will for our lives so that we will know His promises. One of God's promises is that we can ask Him anything and it doesn't matter great or small. God doesn't bless us because we are good, God blesses us because He is good. If you are God's child, then there are no limits to what you can ask.

I love how my youngest son gets in my lap and asks for the craziest things. One thing I do not like is furry animals. Can you guess what he asked for during Christmas one year? A hamster... After I bought the hamster, she escaped out of the cage and roamed her way to my closet. When I saw her in my closet, I screamed and hollered because she scared me. I was so angry that my son was irresponsible for letting the hamster get out and I wanted to get rid of it. However, all I could think about was how sad he looked when the hamster was missing. Consequently, I bought a safer cage for the hamster so that she doesn't get out again. Although I do not like furry animals, I did this all because I love my son.

> *"If you then, evil (sinful by nature) as you are, know how to give good and advantageous gifts to your children, how much more will your Father who is in heaven [perfect as He is] give what is good and advantageous to those who keep on asking Him."* (Matthew 7:11 AMP)

What have you always wanted for your life? What do you day-dream about? What should you be asking God for? I never knew a closed mouth that got fed.

"Ask, and it will be given to you." (John 14:14 NIV)

_____

_____

_____

_____

_____

_____

_____

_____

_____

_____

_____

_____

_____

_____

_____

_____

_____

_____

_____

_____

_____

_____

_____

TRACK 3

LOVE-N-PAIN

LOVE-N-PAIN

*Y*ou can smoke, drink, or find whatever pleases you. However, what's worse, the pain you felt before you self- medicated or the pain from the hangover after?

Am I pretty enough? Did I eat too much? Why didn't I go back to school? Will I ever get married? What's wrong with me?

If you ever find yourself meditating on any harmful questions, then you are bruising yourself. Self-bruising is harmful to the body. The distinct attribute of self-bruising is that it's internal so you can't see it. You can see a physical bruise so you can stop the bleeding or give it attention. However, when you can't see the bruise, then you keep re-injuring the same spot. What happens if you sprain your ankle and keep running? It hurts and prolongs the healing. If you rest it, then it has time to heal properly. What if you try resting your mind to allow your heart to heal properly? Beating yourself up with past regrets or decisions will not fix anything. Are you kind and gentle to others, but criticize yourself?

I love The Golden Rule, *"Do to others what you would have them do to you."* (Matthew 7:12 NIV) However, what if you also tried to do good to yourself so that you can show others how to do good to you also? This will help you to define what your standards are and will keep you from allowing others to hurt you just like you hurt yourself. People prey on insecure people. Love yourself and set the tone how others will treat you. You have a long life ahead of you and God has plans of blessing for your life.

"Eye has not seen, nor ear heard, Nor have entered into the

heart of man The things which God has prepared for those who love Him." (1 Corinthians 2:9 NKJV)

Stop bruising yourself and start loving yourself. The more love you have for yourself, the better you will take care of yourself. Also, the more love you have, the more love you can give. You can't fully love someone else unless you love yourself. Let's start a cycle of love.

What life changes can you make for self-improvement? Instead of meditating on harmful thoughts about your life, why don't you write down what's bothering you and turn those things into positive affirmations. Therefore, instead of your mind racing with negative thoughts, you can use your mouth to speak positive thoughts. Words have authority over thoughts, so those negative thoughts will have to go. How can you take better care of yourself?

"I consider that our present sufferings are not worth comparing with the glory that will be revealed in us."
– (Romans 8:18 NIV)

TRACK 4

SPADES

Ayanna Mills Gallow

SPADES

"With man this is impossible, but with God all things are possible." (Matthew 19:26 NIV)

G rowing up in Freeport, NY, Spades was a household game that we played. Spades consist of four people, two teams, and 52 cards. Each team enters into a bid based on the number of wins they think they can get after each deal. The rules of the game were, Aces were high, deuces were higher and the Jokers were the highest. Whichever team scored the most wins, would win the most points for that hand.

While playing spades, you played to win. The only time you wouldn't play your hand was if you didn't have any spades. Spades was the name of the game so you needed them to play. Well, life is similar. As long as you have breath in your body, then you have life. If you have life, then you can't throw in your hand or give up.

Even if you had low cards and the other team had a better chance of winning, you would still play the game. If they bid eight and you bid five, then it was your goal to make sure they wouldn't get all eight wins while still scoring at least five. If they got seven wins and your team got six, then your team would win because they would get a –80 for not getting eight wins or books and you would get a positive 51 points for getting one more than you expected. Therefore, even though your team knew they didn't have the highest number of cards, they would still play their hand the best they could because there was more than one way to win and defeat the other team.

"Be strong and courageous. Do not be afraid or terrified

because of them, for the Lord your God goes with you; he
will never leave you nor forsake you."
(Deuteronomy 31:6 NIV)

What if we looked at life like that? Maybe we do not have enough money now, but if we manage what we have then we could still achieve our financial goals. Instead of not working as diligent because it doesn't look like you will succeed, what else can you do? What other strategies can you try? Victory in the game of Spades is not based on who wins each hand, but who makes it to 500 first. If the predicted losing team threw their hand in because they feared failure, then they forfeited the game. What are you forfeiting by giving up? What do you need to replace faith with instead of fear?

If you don't throw your hand in, then you may get a 10 for 2 and get to 500 quicker than you thought.

_____

_____

_____

_____

_____

_____

_____

_____

_____

_____

_____

_____

_____

_____

_____

_____

_____

_____

_____

_____

_____

_____

_____

_____

TRACK 5

HYPEMAN

HYPEMAN

"Don't believe the hype. I don't care how many number ones you have at the box office, I don't care how much they say you're great, don't believe it. Just stay in your lane and do what you're supposed to do." – Tyler Perry

"A hype man/hype gall, in hip hop music is a backup rapper and/or singer who supports the primary rappers with exclamations and interjections and who will attempt to increase the audience's excitement with call-and-response chants." (Wikipedia)

Who is your hype man? Who has been supporting you and speaking into your life? Or, who are the naysayers feeding your doubt and insecurities? The questions to ask yourself when deciding someone's purpose in your life are: Do they keep me cold & afraid with negative thoughts that stop my flow? Or, are they helping me warm up with encouragement while pushing me out there waiting to interject if I stumble? Who wins your People's Choice Award? If people are not even in the ranking, then get rid of them STAT!

You are who you hang around. If you hang around successful people, then it will breed success. If you hang around liars, then you are a liar. Even if you tell the truth, hanging around with a liar will label you a liar because perception becomes reality. Therefore, hang around authentic people who will inspire you to soar and who will be there for you if you stumble.

What line would your closest supporters say to you in your time of need? Did they study your lines to help you and interject, or did they study your lines to help you fail.

"Warn a divisive person once, and then warn them a second time. After that, have nothing to do with them."
(Titus 3:10 NIV).

Who are your five favorite hype men dead or alive? Who are the people you need to get rid of? Make a list of who should stay and who should go, and then execute.

"Blessed is the one who does not walk in step with the wicked or stand in the way that sinners take or sit in the company of mockers, but whose delight is in the law of the LORD, and who meditates on his law day and night. That person is like a tree planted by streams of water, which yields its fruit in season and whose leaf does not wither–whatever they do prospers." (Psalms 1:1–3 NIV)

Ayanna Mills Gallow

TRACK 6

DO IT SCARED

TRACK 6
_____

DO IT SCARED

TRACK 7
───────────

FINDING BEAUTY WITHIN

FINDING BEAUTY WITHIN

*A*m I crazy...have you ever asked yourself that? Why can't I be more like him or her? Are you comparing yourself proportionately? Let's look at the facts:

Are you African-American? Did you know that according to statistics, African-American women are two times more likely than white women to be incarcerated? Are you comparing yourself to Lisa who has a father that built a business and lives in a beautiful neighborhood? Does that sound fair? Maybe you should be thankful that you are in the ⅔ of women not incarcerated versus feeling bad because you don't have a degree. Even better, maybe you should be happy to be in the 87% of African-Americans who have a high school education or equivalent. Negative thoughts only weigh you down. If you are going to have a war within, then at least you can fight fair.

According to the United States Census Bureau in November of 2016, 69% of children under 18 live in families with two parents. Did you come from the 31% living in a single parent home comparing yourself to the 69%? You may have not been afforded the same opportunities as them so why would you compare yourself to them? Use the success of others to fuel you to make a difference. If you grew up without one of your parents, then be the best parent you always wanted to your own children. Celebrate your wins. Your life could have turned out so much worse, but it didn't. However, the best thing you have going for yourself, is...the future.

"For I consider that the sufferings of this present time are

Ayanna Mills Gallow | 37

not worthy to be compared with the glory which shall be
revealed in us." (Romans 8:18 NKJV)

Start with an attitude of gratitude. You are talented and God has gifted you with many blessings. Try writing down things that God has done for you. What are you most proud of? What relationships do you value? What do you enjoy doing? Whatever you come up with, be grateful for your story while you strive to make improvements.

TRACK 8

NO LIMITS

NO LIMITS

"Jesus said to him, "If you can believe, all things are possible to him who believes." (Mark 9:23 NKJV)

*R*ule #1– There are no limits. Do not allow anyone to put labels or limitations on you. If you can believe in yourself, then you can achieve what you put your mind too. It's God who put the desire in your heart to do what you are called to do so spend time with God through prayer and reading the Bible. If you have a burning desire to do something, then just go for it!

"Delight yourself in the Lord, and He will give you the desire of your heart." (Psalms 37:4 KJV)

Rule #2– Prepare yourself. Your biggest desires are not going to be average goals. Therefore, you will have to be creative, do your research, and seek wise counsel. No one can do it on their own. Position yourself to be in a winning circle so that you can win. If you plant apple seeds, then you will not grow bananas on the same tree. Bananas do not grow from seeds and they harvest differently than apples. The same way an apple and banana can't be grafted together to grow, is the same way you will not grow with the wrong people. Nonetheless, position yourself in the winning circle so that you can receive your harvest in your due season.

"As long as the earth endures, seed time and harvest, cold and heat, summer and winter, day and night will never cease." (Genesis 8:22 CSB)

#3 Keep Going. If you wanted something ordinary, then it would be easy to get. Therefore, prepare for the battle knowing that challenges will come. No matter what the obstacles are, do not put the limits back on. When runners start a relay race, they do not stop, turn around, and go back the other way. Instead, they look forward with their eye on the finish line and keep running. Stay to the finish and keep running your "own" race to achieve your dreams.

> *"Jesus looked at them and said, With man this is impossible, but with God; all things are possible."* (Matthew 19:26 NIV)

- What are your dreams that you pushed aside due to lack of faith?

- What have you always wanted to do?

- What do you want God to help you achieve?

Take off the limits. What's the worst that could happen?

TRACK 9

KARMA

KARMA

*R*eciprocity refers to a social norm that proves that one positive action results in another positive action. For example, if you are in a room of people and you tell one person to say something positive to another person, then one scenario could be A would tell B something positive and then B would tell A something back positive. Another example is A tells B something positive, then B tells C something positive and then C tells A something positive. Whatever the outcome is, the results will still be A being the receiver of something positive because A was the giver of something positive. The only difference in the two scenarios is the amount of time it took for A to get it back. It can come back directly, or it can be more time in between and come back indirectly.

"Who then is a faithful and wise servant, whom his master made rule over his household, to give them food in due season." (Matthew 24:45 NIV)

You have to wait until it's your season. When a seed is planted in a woman, the best scenario is to give the baby nine months to grow to full-term. As the seed grows, the women prepare the nursery, buys clothes, celebrates the baby's upcoming arrival, starts a college fund and rearranges other priorities. A woman doesn't check for the baby to come out immediately because the baby needs nourishment and time to grow. Therefore, while you are waiting for your harvest, prepare for its arrival and don't get discouraged.

"Let us not become weary in doing good, for at the proper

---

time we will reap a harvest if we do not give up."
(Galatians 6:9 NIV)

While you are waiting for your harvest, keep tilling your land and keep the weeds out. Impatience, anger, discouragement, and negative people are the weeds to keep away from. Keep your investments by continuous water and sunlight. When you water your seed, then you help it grow faster. If you let anger or jealousy get in, then your seed won't get the proper water it needs. Keep your eyes on the sunlight, which comes from the Word of God, so that you can grow while your crop grows.

What are you believing for? How can you sow that into others? Do you want love? If you want love, then put love in the atmosphere so that you can get it back. When you get it back, then put it out some more so that you can get back even more.

"Still other seed fell on good soil, where it produced a crop—a hundred, sixty or thirty times what was sown."
(Matthew 13:8 NIV)

Think about what you want, and figure out a plan to sow it in the form of a seed.

What you put out comes back to you. Therefore, be mindful what you put out because you will see it again.

TRACK 10

HOW DO I GO ON?

HOW DO I GO ON?

*I*t was all a dream... at least it was my dream/fairy tale wedding. The theme of my wedding was horse & carriage/fairy tale. I chose the color purple for royalty, I was carried in by a horse drawn carriage with two white horses. It was at a Chateau which means castle, the cake was topped with a bedazzled horse & carriage as well as the table card holders. It was a magical spring day and to everyone's surprise, it was 77 degrees and sunny after it rained the entire week prior. It was a Sunday morning in New York and the wedding & reception overlooked the South Bay. It was the most beautiful wedding I had ever been too and I was so excited to meet my Prince Charming at the altar. Most important I was so excited because this was the beginning of my happily ever after. God blessed me to bring forth two beautiful and healthy boys and my heart was full.

For my 5th wedding anniversary, my husband had the bright idea to throw me a vow renewal ceremony. It was supposed to be a surprise to me. He reached out to my best friend to help with the cake, he called my parents and asked them to come down, he arranged things with the Pastor who married us originally, and he even had me a beautiful purple dress made by the lady at the church who would make clothes for me. What an excellent idea I thought. After the vow renewal was over, we went to take family pictures and I was very happy.

Our vow renewal was on a Sunday just as our wedding was. On the Tuesday following the renewal, my husband and I planned to stay up late to watch a movie. I fell asleep during the movie and when I woke up he was gone. I called his phone at about 11:00 pm to see where he went. He told me that he went out to check on some work at a club. Working in the evening was not unusual for him because he was a Police Officer turned business owner of a security company. Therefore, a lot of crime happened at night and he had to go. However, this particular night was our special night together and he was supposed to be home. Consequently, when I called him at 1:00 am I was very upset that he still wasn't home.

The next day we had an argument because I was upset that he left. It wasn't a terrible argument or the worse we've had, but he said he didn't want to be married anymore and that he was leaving. I'm thinking, we just renewed our vows three days earlier and said for better or for worse I didn't think this was worse. However, he was very serious and I could not change his mind. The days following, he stayed out even later and I was haunted by the fact that he was leaving me. I didn't know when and I didn't know why. I was distraught, both mentally and physically.

"Weeping may endure for a night, but joy cometh in the morning." (Psalms 30:5 KJV)

Since my husband was leaving me, I gave him a deadline because I knew it wasn't God's will for me to be in a situation like I was in.

"But if the unbeliever leaves, let it be so. The brother or the sister is not bound in such circumstances; God has called us to live in peace." (1 Corinthians 7:15 NIV).

Therefore, I enlisted the help of my family, moved out of the house and turned it into a rental property, and I moved back into an existing property that I had before we got married. I moved across town to be closer to my job and so that it would be easier to manage work and the boys. I prayed and I had others praying for me. I held onto God's Word, *"Fear not, for I am with you; do not be dismayed, for I am your God. I will strengthen you, Yes I will help you, I will uphold you with My righteous right hand."* (Isaiah 41:10 KJV)

God was holding my hand then and He is still holding my hand now. He helped me realize that no matter the situation, good or bad, we always need to trust and lean on Him. God is always available to us when we need him. No matter what we faced or are facing, God will never leave us or fail us. Try turning all of your problems over to God. When I turned mine over to Him, I went from feeling like I wanted to die to believing there were no limits but the sky.

TRACK 11
_____

HOLD ON

HOLD ON

*A*re you always struck with the question, when are you going to have a baby? Or if you have a baby, the question is, "When will you have another? Or, maybe you have two boys like me so the question is, when are you going to get that girl? The answer that I always give is, "Do I have have a choice?"

"Then the Lord God formed a man from the dust of the ground and breathed into his nostrils the breath of life, and the man became a living being." (Genesis 2:7 GNT)

"The Lord will bless you with many children."
(Deuteronomy 28:4 GNT)

God is the one who blesses us with children so we have to wait for Him.

I am too Old

Abraham (Abram) and Sarah (Sarai,) were a couple in the Bible that were promised a son by God. Due to their ages, they doubted God so Abraham decided to have a baby with another woman.

"Haggar bore Abram a son, and he named him Ishmael, Abram was eighty-six years old at the time."
(Genesis: 16:15-16 GNT)

"But God said, "No, Your wife Sarah will bear you a son and you will name him Isaac." (Genesis 17:19 GNT)

"Abraham was a hundred years old when Isaac was born.

Sarah said, "God has brought me joy and laughter."
(Genesis 21:5 (GNT)

Wait on the Lord

Even though Abraham & Sarah moved ahead of God, they still received God's promise. At the age of 100, Abraham had a son named Ishmael, (outside child), and a baby named Isaac (promised heir). If God could bless them after 90 years old, then don't you think He can bless your 40 year old body? Of course this wasn't easy for anyone because Abraham had two children with two different women. Later on, the two brothers would be at war with one another.

The pressure of other people, your age, and other circumstances can be very taxing and make you consider moving ahead of God. However, the sperm bank or a random female is not the answer. God's perfect will is that children be born out of marriage. Regardless if you had children some other way, God will still bless them because everyone and everything made by God is good. However, by trying to decide your own fate, you can cause yourself problems that God never intended you to have.

What Ishmael's can you avoid creating in your life? Should you wait until the time is right to get married? Or wait to start a career? What are you anxiously ready to do, but you don't feel peace about?

"But those who wait on the Lord shall renew their strength;
They shall mount up with wings like eagles, they shall run
and not be weary, they shall walk and faint not."
(Isaiah 40:31 NKJV)

MOM IS GONE

Ayanna Mills Gallow

MOM IS GONE

f you ever had a friend or know someone who lost their mother, then you know how hard it is to watch knowing there is nothing you can do to help. Or perhaps you had a mom who was completely awesome, but she died much earlier than expected. Lastly, maybe you never knew your mother because she died when you were a baby or because she put you up for an adoption; whatever category you may fit in, the resulting factor all leads to grief.

Grief is feelings of heartache, deep sorrow, misery, anguish, and/or pain following the loss of a loved one. Grief is a very powerful emotion that no one else can control, but you. No one can tell you that you should be over it by a certain point. And no one should say, well at least you have such and such or at least this or at least that. Those people usually mean well and they only want to provide comfort. However, grief has to be worked out with the Lord.

"The Lord is close to the brokenhearted and saves those who are crushed in spirit." (Psalms 34:18 NIV)

God says, *"Cast all your anxiety on him because he cares for you."* (1 Peter 5:7 NIV) Grief can feel unbearable and everlasting, but God still wants us to have joy. *"To be away from the body and at home with the Lord."* (2 Corinthians 5:8 NIV). Because we know the late mothers are present with the Lord, we know they are okay and their spirit lives. We can find great cheer because we will see them again.

"For the Lord Himself will descend from heaven with a shout, with the voice of an archangel, and with the trumpet of God.

*And the dead in Christ will rise first. Then we who are alive
and remain shall be caught up together with them in the
clouds to meet the Lord in the air. And thus we shall always
be with the Lord."* (I Thessalonians 4:16–17 NAS.)

Therefore, focus, (encourage others to focus), on the mere fact
that we will see them again. Until that time comes, cherish their memories and the good times. Controlling your thoughts and focusing on
good memories give you peace.

Life can feel unnatural to have a mother gone too soon or not
to know a mother's love at all. Even with that, God is with you and
you will get through it. Lean on God's love and know that He has not
left you alone. Know this, *"It is the Lord who goes before you; He will
be with you. He will not fail you or abandon you."* (Deuteronomy 38:8
AMP)

Rest In Peace: Ms. Felicia Denise Daniels, Ms. Ketta Aydelott, and
Ms. Sharon Elizabeth Sutton.

TRACK 13
─────────────

PREGNANT DAUGHTER

.

PREGNANT DAUGHTER

"Judge carefully, for with the Lord our God there is no injustice or partiality or bribery." (2 Chronicles 19:7)

Poem on the beginning of My Life- Ayanna Mills Gallow
When I think of my life, I thank God for sustaining me.
He really had a plan and it was His purpose I came to be.
Born to a 13-year-old girl
Lost in this very cold world.

Absent of guidance and forced to deal with the circumstance
Filled with fear but she still decided to give my life a chance.
A baby girl born with traits of someone she viewed as a monster
She still committed her life to me and didn't let anyone put asunder.
It was tough and she had to face her pain by looking at me every day
But she didn't let her dark days or depression take her away.
She dealt with the hand that she was dealt
Others looked down on her but had no idea the pain she felt.
Raped by a man who was supposed to be a father
No wonder my mere existence was a constant bother.
She didn't only have me to remind her of the pain day to day
She still had to see her monster because my grandmother still gave
him a place to stay.
Forgiveness, love, survival are things my grandmother did honor
But she forgot about the pain this was causing her daughter.
I will never judge the reasons why she let him stay
But because he was around I had somebody there for play.

My mother carried pain because of this
But when I couldn't see him, his face I did miss.

He did something so wrong to my mother
But it's like a catch 22 because he was my father.
I knew him as grandad and his name I always yelled
But the pain he caused is the reason for the alcohol I always smelled.
He drank and drank to wash his pain away
This led to his downfall and in the grave his body does lay.
I loved him so much and can't deny that he paved the way
Although he was drunk, on the weekends games we would play.
He would teach me to "think face" and we would race down the street
But then he would get sad and say, "Do you think your mother hates me?"
I would say, no granddaddy she doesn't hate you
He would feel better and say she should be glad she has you.
I knew the problems between them had nothing to do with me
But if my grandmother did kick him out, then his face I wouldn't have been able to see.

God has a reason why He lets things be
I thank God my mother has found him and learned to appreciate me.
If it wasn't for her than I wouldn't be able to write this book today
She gave me the drive because she taught me education could never be taken away
She led me to go to school and then back for my masters
And she wouldn't allow me around people unless they possessed a certain character.
I can't believe my mom raised me with the pain she had to face
But although we were close in age, she had no problem putting me in my place
I love my mom and thank God she raised me this way.
Even though I was born just 6 weeks after her 13th birthday.
So whenever you see a 13 year old with a baby
Don't think of her as crazy
When you see a young girl pregnant or with a baby, don't make the person feel ashamed. Think about my mom and that it was her step

father to blame.

Judgment:

Who do you need to stop judging? Who do you need to practice forgiveness with? What is holding you back? How can you deal with those issues like my mother eventually did by turning them over to God?

TRACK 14

CASE DISMISSED

CASE DISMISSED

*D*o you think people make a conscious decision to live lawlessly? Are the people who break the law bad people? If they bring it on themselves, then do they deserve a negative recourse? I believe anyone can turn their life around and that everyone deserves more than one chance.

> *The Lord said to Samuel, "Don't judge by his appearance or height, for I have rejected him. The Lord doesn't see things the way you see them. People judge by the outward appearance, but the Lord looks at the heart."*
> (1 Samuel 16:7 NIV)

We are all similar. We all want love, good relationships and a feeling of relevancy. Sometimes people make bad choices because of the lack of one or all of those things. It's easy to have compassion on someone who has a terminal sickness because they didn't ask to be sick. However, do you think your brother or sister asked to be a drug addict, alcoholic, whoremonger, or lawbreaker?

> *"Blessed are those whose lawless deeds are forgiven, and whose sins are covered."* (Romans 4:7 NKJV).

The thing about drugs and alcohol is that there are programs to help people get free of the problem. There is help for them because the problem is defined. However, you can't define a drug dealer's problems. You can't define why a person keeps breaking the law. Perhaps the law breaker lacked the love, relationships, or the relevance feelings that led to a downward spiral of events. Instead of tough love, let's just try love. *"So as God's own chosen people, who are holy and well-beloved, put on a heart of compassion kindness, humility, gen-tleness, and patience."* (Colossians 3:12 AMP). Therefore, instead of saying, "He or she brought it on himself," think about what he or she lacked that led him or her in the wrong direction. Once you stop judging by what it looks like on the outside, then you will be able to show compassion.

Don't judge a book at first glance. The story gets better over time if you give it a chance.

TRACK 15
_____

CONTRIBUTIONS

Ayanna Mills Gallow

CONTRIBUTIONS

*W*hat do you bring to the table? Don't come to the table just to eat, come to the table to see who you can reach.

Whose life are you contributing too? What child/children are you investing in? What if I told you that the second leading cause of death for children ages 15-24 is suicide? Would you increase your investment in children then?

*"The single most common factor for children who develop resilience is at least **one** stable and committed relationship with a supportive parent, caregiver or adult."* (Josh Shipp- The Grown-Up's Guide to Teenage Humans)

Divorce, death, bullying, loneliness, learning disabilities, health challenges, feelings of inadequacy, and so many other factors affect children. Children need reassurance that they will overcome any obstacle they face. As an adult, we have a responsibility to reinforce God's Word that says, *"Being confident of this, He who began a good work in you will carry it on to completion until the day of Christ Jesus."* (Philippians 1:6 NIV) Consequently, they will understand that problems will come, but they have so much more life to live.

At the age of eight, my oldest son developed test anxiety as he prepared for a milestone exam. This landed him in the Emergency room with stomach pain as the test approached. I told him if he failed, then it's not the end of the world. His response to me was, "Yes it is." That was a major eye opener for me. However, I am happy he expressed his feelings because he did fail the test.

What if I didn't comfort him with love and support prior to the test? What if I never knew how he felt about the test? As a mother it is my job to spend time with my children so that I can be the voice they hear when times are tough. Even if you do not have children, God still wants you to add stability to some child's life.

> *"And whoever welcomes one such child in my name welcomes me."* (Matthew 18:5 NIV)

Unfortunately, suicide is a leading cause of death among people ages 15 to 24 in the US (Melonie Herron, 2018). It is very alarming that the world can seem so unbearable and suicide can seem like a better option. Thank God Eminem didn't get caught in the suicide group. If he had, then so many children would not benefit from his Marshall Mathers Foundation which is a charity to help disadvantaged youth in his home state of Michigan. Music helped him discover he had a bigger purpose. What can you help a child discover?

Whose life are you contributing too? What can you do to decrease the suicide rate? No child should feel like there life is not wanted.

_____

_____

_____

_____

_____

_____

_____

_____

_____

_____

_____

_____

_____

_____

_____

_____

_____

_____

_____

_____

_____

_____

TRACK 16

MY GIFT

MY GIFT

*M*y biggest blessing in life is being a mom to my sons. It is not an easy job, but it is my favorite job. My decisions must consider what's in their best interest. I owe them my love, time, and guidance.

Children are a gift from the Lord and parenthood should be a joy to us. God entrusted us with our children, so we have to teach our gift, protect our gift, love our gift, and develop our gift. We owe it to our children to teach them how to survive and thrive in this journey called life. *"Train up a child in the way he should go and when he is older he will not depart from it."* (Proverbs 22:6 NKJV) What are the things you don't want your child to depart from when he is older? Whatever those things are requires training on your part. Here are the principles I don't want my children to depart from:

1. God created us for His purpose and His plan is for us to be prosperous and in health. (Jeremiah 29:11)

2. God loves us so much that He sent Jesus so that we could have an abundant life. (John 3:16); (John 10:10)

3. Nothing can separate us from the love of God. (Romans 8:38)

How do you train a child to know that? You initiate prayer as early as possible. Even if they are too young to talk, then you teach them to lift their hands starting when they wake up in the morning. When I used to pick my son Colby up out of his crib, I would say, "Thank you God for waking us up this morning." Then he would raise his hands in the air. Although he couldn't talk, he understood that lifting our hands up to God was a form of thanks. Once he was around two years old, then he would actually say the words.

It was important for me to teach him to do this early in the morning so that I could teach him to start off his day by praising God and recognizing that it's God who woke us up. Once he could talk fluently, then we started having prayer and then his baby brother would later be the one lifting his hands when he saw me in the morning until he could talk. It starts with teaching them as early as possible. *"Those that seek me early shall find me."* (Jeremiah 29:13 KJV)

It is never too late and you can start at any age. What can you teach your children that will benefit them for a lifetime? What are the top five things you want your children to learn from you? How can you be creative to teach those principles?

Children do not respond the best to the old saying, "Do what I say." They respond better to, do as I do. What is your life's plan on being a good parent?

TRACK 17

CHILDREN ARE OUR FUTURE

CHILDREN ARE OUR FUTURE

*W*hat are you teaching your children? What are the core principles you enforce on a daily basis? What do you wish you learned when you were growing up?

Both prayer and love are very important and should be taught to our children. These are two principles that can help them with every aspect of life. As parents, if we know this, then we should make sure it's embedded in them.

Prayer

"Do not be anxious about anything, but in everything by prayer and supplication with thanksgiving let your requests be made known to God." (Philippians 4:6).

You should teach your children to pray because nothing gets done without prayer. God sees all things and knows all things to come, but He will not force His will on us. Teach your children to ask God for protection from all unforeseen evil and for preparation for all things to come. When you teach children to ask God for help, not only does it let them know they are not alone, but also that God is in control. God is with them every second and they have access to Him 24/7. Why not ask Him for help? If they have fear concerning anything, then they should go to God first. As parents we want to protect our children from trouble. However, we have to teach the children to look out for themselves by their prayers. Teach them to rely on God.

Love

"And now these three remain: faith, hope and love. But the greatest of these is love." (1 Corinthians 13:13).

One way to teach them love is to reject negative conversations concerning others. Set an example so that they won't become bullies and talk negative about others. Reject all negative gossip and discord. God loves people who behave both good and bad and He is not a respector of person. It's important that they know to respect everybody not because they are behaving good, but because they were made by God and everything made by God is good. God loves all His children and we can show that by extending love. Love is shown by example.

What does your love look like?

Do your children see you smiling at people? Are you helping others? Are you kind to people? Are you loving on your children? Do you congratulate and encourage them? What are you doing to show love to them and others?

"Love is patient, love is kind. It does not envy, it does not boast, it is not proud. It does not dishonor others, it is not self-seeking, it is not easily angered, it keeps no record of wrongs. Love does not delight in evil but rejoices with the truth. It always protects, always trusts, always hopes, always perseveres. Love never fails." (1 Corinthians 13:4–8)

GREATNESS COMMANDMENTS

GREATNESS COMMANDMENTS

*I*n order to be successful, you have to plan. God wants you to go far in life and He created you so that you can be successful, influential, and help your brothers and sisters to do the same. However, in order to achieve your greatness, you have to, "Write your vision, and make it plain." When you put your plan in writing, it helps you to stay on track. Here are some tips to help you with planning your journey for greatness:

Nine Tips to your path of Greatness

1. **Greeting:** Greet everyone with a smile on your face and a firm handshake while looking them in the eye. Your greeting is also a way to sell yourself. Have a short 30-second speech prepared that accentuates your best qualities. Have it rehearsed and while saying it, envision the person you are talking to as a connection that will lead to your success. Everyone you greet and meet is important so be prepared. Be prepared for everything always.

2. **Research:** whenever you have a job interview or a meeting with others that you do not know, then prepare in advance by researching the person and or company. Linkedin and social media are great ways to do this because everyone in business should have some form of internet presence.

3. **Everyone:** Everyone you meet is important. There are 7 Degrees of separation and you never know who you are talking too. From the janitor to the ceo, treat everyone with kindness

and grace.

"Do not forget to show hospitality to strangers, for by doing some have shown hospitality to angels without knowing it."
-(Hebrews 13:2 NIV)

4. **Association:** Associate yourself with other great people. Be around positive people not the naysayers.

"My son, do not walk in the way with them, Keep your foot from their path." (Proverbs 1:15 NKJV)

5. **Teach** others the hard lessons that you've learned. After you make traction in your career or figure out your key to life, then give back by helping others.

"Give, and it will be given to you: good measure, pressed down, shaken together, and running over will be put into your bosom. For with the same measure that you use, it will be measured back to you." (Luke 6:38 NKJV)

6. **Never** give up. Attack everything with confidence and bold-ness. Confidence is your brand even if you do not feel confi-dent. Even if you get a no, keep going. A delay is not a deny and a no does not mean never. Never give up on your dreams.

"I can do all this through him who gives me strength."
(Philippians 4:13 NIV)

7. **Education:** Educate yourself and plan for your success. Learn what steps you need to take to achieve your goal. Designa-tions or certifications get acquainted with it and go get it!

"For as the body without the spirit is dead, so faith without works is dead also." (James 2:26 NKJV)

8. **Smiling:** Smile more when you are feeling down or discouraged. We know that smiling tricks your body and increases your endorphins so that you are happy. Smiling should be daily because you know that everything will work out good.

"And we know that all things work together for good to those who love God, to those who are the called according to His purpose." (Romans 8:28 NKJV)

9. **Speak Life:** Speak positive things about yourself. You are what you say you are and what you say is what will happen. Fill the atmosphere with good affirmations and declarations.

"The tongue has the power of life and death and those who love it will eat its fruit." (Proverbs 18:21 NIV)

What are some things you can do to put these tips into practice? How can you prepare better for your success? I encourage you to review each tip, with prayer, and apply it to your life.

_____

_____

_____

_____

_____

_____

_____

_____

_____

_____

_____

_____

_____

_____

_____

_____

_____

_____

_____

_____

_____

_____

_____

_____

_____

THE RULES OF THE GAME

Ayanna Mills Gallow

THE RULES OF THE GAME

*I*n the Game of Chess, a Queen is a very powerful piece. The Queen has the most flexibility and the most moves. The Queen piece can move in any one direction as far as possible. The Queen is the strongest piece so the goal of the Pawn, a less superior piece, is to be promoted to Queen. When the Pawn reaches the 8th rank, then that piece gets promoted to Queen. The Queen stays in the game as long as she doesn't capture an opponent's piece. If she does, then her move is over.

What if you applied the above rules of Chess to your life?

Promotion:

What is a Queen? A Queen is a woman of excellence who operates with morality and integrity. A Queen can be a First Lady, Mother, Grandmother, Auntie, and Community Leader. What if you, male or female, act in a way to be an example of excellence to someone else? What if you display positive strength to help someone aspire to be like you such as the Pawn to the Queen?

Collaboration:

Instead of competing against your brother and sister, what if you collaborate with them. Doing this can benefit you and them. What if you partnered with someone?

"Two are better than one, because they have a good return

---

for their labor If either of them falls down, one can help the other up." (Ecclesiastes 4:9–10 NIV)

Maybe you could volunteer and assist someone who is doing something you desire to do? By this, you not only help them, but you also gain wisdom regarding their experiences.

Cooperation:

In Chess, the Queen can move to any unoccupied spaces, but the Queen's move is over when she captures an opponent's piece. As long as she cooperates with the rules, then she stays on board. How much more could you win if you cooperated versus following your own rules? If you cooperate and do the things you know you should, then you can stay on board versus end something that could have been a win for you.

Here are some self-reflection questions for you to consider:

- Do you have someone that you look up too? If not, then you need to change your circle.

- Who are the people you want on your team to help you go to the next level?

- How can you be a role model for others?

JUSTIFYING WRONGS

JUSTIFYING WRONGS

S lavery is a part of the past. Don't make jail a part of your future. Live your life freely.

> *"The earth is the Lord's, and everything in it, the world, and all who live in it; for he founded it on the seas and established it on the waters."* (Psalm 24: 1-2 NIV)

God created the world and He gave us the Bible as our instruction manual for life. We should use the Bible as a guide for our behaviors and our actions. Since God is the creator, why not go to him for counsel concerning how to handle the police?

> *"Submit yourselves for the Lord's sake to every human authority: whether to the emperor, as the supreme authority, or to the governors, who are sent by him to punish those who do wrong and to commend those who right. For it is God's will that by doing good you should silence the ignorant talk of foolish people."* (1 Peter 2:13- 15 NIV)

Submission does not equal agreement. Submission means that you are being obedient, compliant, non-resisting, and respectful. God instructed us to submit to all those in authority. All includes parents, teachers, police officers, government officials, and whoever else is in charge. We may not like everything they do, but we shouldn't be disrespectful. I didn't like everything my mom told me to do as a child, but I wouldn't talk back or mumble under my breath in front of her. If I had, then she would have taken it as me trying to be the boss. I did not want that because nothing good would have come out of my disobedience. Therefore, we have to give honor to whom is due.

Feeling powerless is a common factor that leads to anger. One physical effect of anger is that it can trigger the body's fight or flight response. Therefore, if a person lawfully holds the power and you make him feel powerless, then what will be the resulting factor? Although we are not responsible for anyone else's actions, we can do our best not to provoke them. Keep in mind, if an officer responds unlawfully, then he will have to give an account. However, it's our job to submit, resist all urges to get upset, and to get back home safely to our families.

"Pride goes before destruction." (Proverbs 16: 18 NIV). Pride can make you feel like responding with disobedience when wrongfully accused or profiled. I teach my sons that if a police officer ever pulls them over, then they should respond with, "Yes sir or yes ma'am. Therefore, submit and wait until you get your time to speak which should be in front of other witnesses and law officials. A conflict resolution in the bible says, *"But if they will not listen, take one or two others along, so that every matter may be established by the testimony of two or three witnesses."* (Matthew 18:16 NIV) Therefore, on the side of the road is not the place to plead your case because it's your word against there's.

I know there is injustice in the world, but it's not worth your life, freedom, or the heartache it would cause your loved ones. I want to give some tips to live more peaceful with those in authority and any difficult people you may encounter.

Tactics for feeling disrespected or wrongfully accused:

1. Remember that feelings are temporary and subject to changes. Make a decision to replace those negative feelings with positive thoughts.

2. Give the most authentic smile that you can. When you smile, it releases endorphins and tricks your brain to think you are happy. Smiling benefits your health and actually decreases your blood pressure. Instead of confrontation it can actually dissolve something. It also lets the person know that you have control over your emotions.

3. Look for the good in the person. Ask yourself, why are they saying that? What happened to them so bad that made them want to bring others to their misery party? Misery does love company, but what or who hurt this person so bad that made them want to hurt me? This can actually help you to pity the person and get you to show more compassion. Kill them with kindness.

4. Understand that God has a purpose for you and see the big picture versus what is happening at the time. Be big minded and not caught up in the moment.

Don't think about who's wrong or who has the right a way.
Think about your life and seeing your family another day.
Think smart.

TRACK 21

THE SPIRIT OF
EXCELLENCE

THE SPIRIT OF EXCELLENCE

*W*hat grade did you make in school? Were you a B student striving for A's or a C student content with C's? Was your goal to be at the top or was your goal to benefit from the curve? Where were you then versus where you want to be now?

Grading on a curve is a method teachers use to grade tests. Usually, grading on a curve increases a student's grade. One method of curve grading is, if the highest grade on a test was an 85. Then the teacher would subtract 85 from 100, since no one received a perfect score, and then add the difference to everyone's score. Therefore, instead of 100 being the highest score, 85 is converted to 100.

When I took Statistics in college, my classmates would get mad because they would say that I messed up the curve. Meaning, if I would had received and 80, then the professor would have added 20 additional points to everyone else's grade because I received the highest grade. However, because I received a 90, then they would only get additional 10 points added to their grade. In my opinion, curve grading doesn't adequately assess one's knowledge; Curve grading promotes slackness.

In the Bible, Daniel was a real stand up man with a spirit of excellence. As a result, Daniel was promoted. Although Daniel was blameless, he was still persecuted. However, Daniel persevered and remained faithful to God. When you operate in the spirit of excellence, then you win and excel in life no matter the obstacles. Let's look at Daniel:

1. **Promotion**– "Now Daniel so distinguished himself among the administrators and the satraps by his exceptional qualities that the king planned to set him over the whole kingdom." (Daniel 6:3 NIV)

2. **Praying Man**– "He knelt down on his knees three times that day, and prayed and gave thanks before his God, as was his custom since early days. (Daniel 3:10 NKJV)

3. **Favor & Divine Protection**– "Now the king was exceedingly glad for him, and commanded that they should take Daniel up out of the den. So Daniel was taken up out of the den, and no injury whatever was found on him, because he believed his God." (Daniel 6:23 NKJV)

4. **Prosperity**–"So this Daniel prospered in the reign of Darius and in the reign of Cyrus the Persian." (Daniel 6:28 NIV)

5. **Vengeance**–"At the King's command, the men who had falsely accused Daniel were brought in and thrown into the lions' den, along with their wives and children." (Daniel 6:24 NIV)

Therefore, Daniels persistence, perseverance, prayers, and loyalty earned him favor, protection, and prosperity regardless of persecution. Do you want to operate in excellence like Daniel, or will you look at someone else to miss the maximum mark so that you can get the points as in curve grading?

BONUS TRACK

PRAY TO MAKE IT TODAY

Ayanna Mills Gallow

PRAY TO MAKE IT TODAY

*W*hen you know God's Word and you can recite it back through prayer, then you get a certain level of peace. The peace you receive is powerful because when you say the Word during prayer, then your faith increases. "So then faith comes by hearing, and hearing by the word of God." (Romans 10:17) I challenge you to pray these scriptures during your time with God so that your faith will be unwavering concerning each area listed below.

God's Plan:

"For I know the plans I have for you," declares the LORD, "plans to prosper you and not to harm you, plans to give you hope and a future." (Jeremiah 29:11)

"What then shall we say to these things? If God is for us, who can be against us? He who did not spare His own Son, but delivered Him up for us all, how shall He not with Him also freely give us all things?" (Romans 8:31–32)

Wisdom:

"If any of you lack wisdom, let him ask of God, that giveth to all men liberally, and upbraideth not; and it shall be given him." (James 1:5)

"If you ask anything in My name, I will do it." (John 14:14)

Health & Prosperity:

"I know thy works: behold, I have set before thee an *open door*, and no man can shut it: for thou hast a little strength, and hast kept my word, and hast not denied my name." (Revelation 3:8)

"This book of the law shall not depart out of thy mouth; but thou shalt meditate therein day and night, that thou mayest observe to do according to all that is written therein: for then thou shalt make thy way *prosperous*, and then thou shalt have good success." (Joshua 1:8)

"Beloved, I wish above all things that thou mayest *prosper* and be *in health*, even as thy soul prospereth." (3 John 1:2)

SALVATION:

"That if you confess with your mouth the Lord Jesus and believe in your heart that God has raised Him from the dead, you will be saved." (Romans 10:9)

"This is the confidence we have in approaching God: that if we ask anything according to his will, he hears us. And if we know that he hears us—whatever we ask—we know that we have what we asked of him." (1 John 5:14-15)

_____

_____

_____

_____

_____

_____

_____

_____

_____

_____

_____

_____

_____

_____

_____

_____

_____

_____

_____

_____

_____

_____

_____

_____

_____

BIBLIOGRAPHY

Ready to Die. (1994). On *Ready to Die*. Label: Bad Boy.

Hold On. (2000). On *Notorious K.I.M*. Label: Atlantic Records.

I'm Goin' Down. (1995). On *My Life*. Label: Uptown, MCA.

Broadside, B. (n.d.). The 50th Anniversary of Martin Luther King, Jr.'s, "What Is Your Life's Blueprint?"

I Believe I Can Fly. (1996). On *Space Jam: Music from and Inspired by the Motion Picture*. Label: Atlantic Jive.

Melonie Herron, P. D. (2018). *Deaths: Leading Causes for 2016*.

Movement Stop The Violence Self Destruction [Sound Recording]. – [s.l.] : Label Jive, 1989.

NAACP. (n.d.). *Criminal Justice Fact Sheet*. Retrieved from naacp.org: www.naacp.org/criminal-justice-fact-sheet/

Perry, T. (n.d.). *AZ Quotes*. Retrieved from azquotes.com.

Shipp, J. (2017). *The Grown-Up's Guide to Teenage Humans*. HarperCollins.

AUTHOR BIOGRAPHY

Bio: Life & Times of AMG
Artist: Ayanna Mills Gallow
Release Date: April 21st
Genre: God, Gospel, Hip Hop, Gangster Rap
Birth Place: New York

Ayanna grew up as an only child in Freeport, New York. Because of being an only child, she values her relationships with other people which inspired her to join Alpha Kappa Alpha Sorority, Incorporated.

In High School, Ayanna was inducted into the National Honors Society. After 2 years in college, she was also promoted to the Honors Program. She attended Temple University in Philadelphia, Pennsylvania for 4 years where she graduated Magna Cum Laude with a Bachelor's of Business and Administration. She graduated with a dual major in Marketing and Risk Management & Insurance. 4 years later, Ayanna obtained her Masters of Business and Administration from Mercer University in Atlanta, Georgia in while working full time. Since graduating from undergrad, Ayanna has enjoyed a career in the Insurance Industry.

Ayanna has studied Christianity principles for over 15 years. Her Christian beliefs in conjunction with the success she received in business inspired her desire to help others. Her passion is for people to work together to achieve career advancement, educational goals, and community outreach. She serves on the Board of Directors for Women of Integrity, Incorporated. Her strengths are harmonization, goal focused, and result driven. Her principles are based on faith in God and His plans for her to live a blessed life.

Ayanna grew up watching her mother be an overachiever, which she emulated. Her mother has been an intricate part of Ayanna's life & success. She laughs because her mother tells her that, "Her brain is like a computer." Ayanna's two biggest accomplishments & investments in life are her sons, Colby Jacob & Caleb Sterling. She enjoys watching them sing and perform to old hip hop music. They are the loves & joys of her life.